THE SEVEN DEADLY SINS OF INNOVATION

MAT SHORE

INDEX

Printed in the United Kingdom
This edition 2017

Mat Shore LTD
28 Abbey Road, Chertsey, KT16 8AL
www.MatShore.com
matshore@matshore.com
Subscribe to Mats' YouTube Channel: MatShoreInnovation

INTRODUCTION:
WHY I HATE BUYING BOOKS AT AIRPORTS

It's all in the telling...

Just over 10 years ago, I switched from my comfortable career in brand management at Procter & Gamble, Pepsi and Unilever to go it alone as an innovation consultant. My first encounter was a client who told me he wanted to generate insights and value propositions. Within 5 minutes it was clear that he didn't have a clue what that entailed, how it would be done or even what success looked like at the end.

All around me I saw consultancies, agencies and 'gurus' hiding their own lack of understanding behind buzzwords and complex methodologies. With everyone confused, at the end of each project, the client was inevitably left with an unusable report, some pretty concept boards and a huge bill to explain to their boss.

I suppose it was at that moment that I realised that baffling the client was a mug's game. Instead I needed to offer help in aligning the basic language, principles and approach.

There was however no training on 'What is an insight?' and 'How do I write and test a value proposition to see if a new product should proceed?' So I needed to write one.

My disadvantage was, not only had I never written training before, but I was the worst training participant on earth. I hated being lectured, I hate Venn Diagrams with a passion and I despise trainers who are simply reading from the same PowerPoint slide I am. My philosophy had always been if you want that kind of stuff 'Go buy a book in an airport bookshop'. Training needs to be entertaining, interactive and utterly compelling to hold my attention. My torture test for any training would have to be' Would I sit through this?', which is a tough test indeed...

So it was, that I set about creating a training course on the key question of how to create insights and value propositions. I ensured that whenever there was principle to be taught, there were entertaining true stories to back them up.

I quickly learned that the more outrageous and ridiculous the bad examples, the more effectively people learned what not to do. The more elegant and simple the good examples, the more they saw why they needed to change. Equally if what I'm saying is true, I shouldn't have just one example, but hundreds.

Here we are a decade later and I've personally trained 35,000 people. I've trained the board rooms of the worlds biggest technology companies right through to the smallest start ups. It's hugely satisfying when someone comes up to me at an airport and says. 'I loved your training. I always tell people your story about the whale, the dream programmer, or the iron that phones you at work". They never say, I so loved your Venn diagrams!

More and more nowadays I'm invited to go into companies at the request of someone I've trained years back, who wants me to explain the principles to a new generation. The request is always the same 'Make sure you use those great examples', and of course I'm never short of those.

Over the years its been suggested that I write these principles down in a book, but the idea of writing something that ends up in an airport book shop fills me with dread. So I've written this book, like I wrote my training, full of stories that make you laugh, but sneakily teach you something at the same time. And I guarantee there are no diagrams to be found!!!

Mat Shore

Mat Shore
Marketing Consultant

INSPIRING
INNOVATION

THE SEVEN DEADLY SINS OF INNOVATION - WHY WE ARE ALL SINNERS

When friends ask me what I actually teach people, I say:

"I tell companies that they should ask people what they want before making something!"

The usual response is, "Surely they know that already? How do you make a living from pointing out the bleeding obvious?"

I guess what casual observers are missing is that in most industries, its not obvious at all. Many companies are actually structured in a way that makes my 7 sins of innovation inevitable.

Take the Dream Programmer I mentioned. Here was a team in a big company who invited me in to discuss a new innovation they had developed. Honestly, they really had developed a product which allowed you to pick your dreams. Want to Jet ski with Brad Pitt? Done. Learn Needle Craft with Taylor Swift? It's yours.

They were so proud of themselves, it had taken years to develop and they were ready to come to market. Strangely, only now were they considering the insight and value proposition?

So my first question as always was, "Who asked you for that?", to which the reply came "No one". I rapidly followed up with "Then why have you done it?", to which the response came "Because we could".

There's a great scene in Jurassic Park where Jeff Goldbloom and Richard Attenborough have the following exchange. "I don't think you're giving us our due credit. Our scientists have done things which nobody's ever done before... "

"Yeah, yeah, but your scientists were so preoccupied with whether or not they could that they didn't stop to think if they should. "

In many companies, the truth is that engineering and product development are so complex that it takes years of working on something to find out whether it's even possible. Only then do teams begin to wonder, whether or not it has an application. Most often by this point, the idea has become a costly monster with a momentum of its own or the pet project of a senior manager who's career is inextricably linked to it coming to market.

As I said in a recent Times interview, in most companies launching something is easy. It is stopping something coming to market that's nigh on impossible!

I was once told that I misunderstood the role of marketing and product management. "Its not driven by what the market needs ", I was told passionately, "Its role is to retrospectively back-fit an explanation against what the company was going to do anyway!"

Perhaps that's why we all become sinners in the end and why so many innovations fail!

I can list you hundreds, maybe thousands of utterly pointless innovations I've encountered, from pills that tan you from the inside, to an iPad based potty for your toddlers. This book is full of innovation sinners who were tempted into believing they could create a need that didn't exist.

Somehow they believe that their sins will not catch them out. The vast attrition rate of failed innovations and wasted investment is something that always happens to someone else.

The good news is that over the years I've proven that insights and complex technologies are not incompatible. In this book I'll show you the best way to use these principles to repent the sins of retrofitting and start becoming customer insight driven.

BREAK THE CYCLE

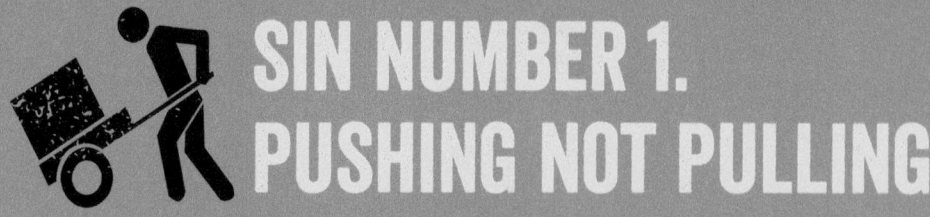

SIN NUMBER 1.
PUSHING NOT PULLING

Why no one ever needed a drill...

When I talk to clients about the first deadly Sin of Innovation and the danger of developers pushing their ideas to the market, I often make reference to the following analogy: nobody ever needed a drill; what they needed was a hole.

The saying may have been around since the 1940s, but it remains just as true today as it did then. You see, if developers fail to recognise the difference between the drill and the hole, they end up creating a form of innovation that is not insight driven.

What do I mean by this? Well, consider the following scenario:

A drill manufacturer, keen to extend their product offering, asks the customer 'how can we improve the drills we already make?' The customer, contemplating the existing type of drill, may say something like *"maybe you could make it longer / thinner / shorter / wider; maybe put various sizes of the drill in a box to give more choice? How about introducing a way of hanging the drill on a ladder so it's in easy reach while I'm working?"*

It may seem like the manufacturer is generating insight, but the only action they will perform as a result of this process is the creation of another drill. Also everyone in this scenario seems utterly bewildered when the competition develop the same improvements! Why? The competition invariably asked the same customer the exact same questions and got the exact same answers.

Now consider this approach: Instead of asking the customers about the current solution (The drill), the manufacturer asks about the desired outcome; *"Why do you need to make a hole?"*

Moving the focus away from the drill, the customer may respond with something like *"I've just redecorated a room in my house and now I want to hang some pictures up".*

What the customer actually needs is a way of hanging the pictures that is secure, yet won't leave any damage to the walls. The manufacturer, armed with true insight, can now go away and develop a solution. (Which is likely to be different from a drill!)

Put simply, asking about the desired outcome is far more likely to lead to breakthrough innovation. It's obvious when you think about it, so why do so many companies fail to do this?

In my experience, a company that has expertise in a specific product won't really want to consider alternative solutions. They have a vested interest in making sure that any consumer 'insight' will build on the original product. It's not that these companies don't know how to ask different questions; it's more that they don't want to ask different questions.

I've lost count of the amount of times I've witnessed companies kicking themselves, asking; "why didn't we see that coming? Why didn't we understand what the customer wanted?" As I often find
myself saying to these organisations, it's because your research and 'customer insight' was steered in a way that demanded your existing technology. Indeed a contradictory customer response would have been hugely inconvenient.

There is no rule that says big companies succeed in their innovation by divine right. Indeed statistics show that 80% of all innovation fails to achieve its launch objectives and is removed from market.

When studies have looked at why innovation fails, its not the quality of the product, or lack of distribution. No, the single biggest reason is that customers do not understand what value it adds. The company is selling a drill and they are looking to buy a hole.

BREAKTHROUGH

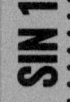 **SIN 1** **PUSHING NOT PULLING**
Selling the drill not the hole.
Thinking about what you want to make, not what others need.

> **"EVEN THE SLICKEST TECHNOLOGY CAN'T OVERCOME THE LACK OF A VALUE PROPOSITION"**

CASE STUDY SIN #1
 – APPLE WATCH

Pushing not Pulling...

In every training I do, in every blog I write on the subject of customer insight, someone is always bound to trot out the same tired objection. " Ford said that consumers don't know what they want and would have asked for a faster horse" or "Steve Jobs didn't believe in customer opinion, Apple created needs when it created the iPad".

This of course is nonsense, but is a helpful belief system that legitimises everyone out there with a secret innovation god complex . It validates those little whispers in their head that says "Don't worry that no one needs it, build it and they will come!"

For every Apple iPad there are tens of thousands of Segway's, Nintendo U's and Crystal Pepsi's. Innovations created by big grown up, clever companies who also felt that they could push not pull.

Even within Apple, a company with a relatively small portfolio of products there has been the odd Newton, Apple Maps and Siri to suggest that not everything it touches is golden.

Its biggest successes have also built on the shoulders and market research of others, who initially developed the proposition. Think iPod. Many consumers and product managers share a revisionists view of history that Apple invented the MP3 player. For those of you like me who owned early mp3 players, you will realise that that Apple refined rather developed that solution. Similarly Apple were not the first company to think of the tablet computer, the TV media streamer, the mp3 store, the laptop, the home computer nor the smart phone.

When you think about it like this, it sheds a new light on the suggestion that famously shunning market research and insight development worked for Apple.

A better question would be, what new breakthrough platforms and innovations did this absence of insight create?

Which brings me to the folly which is the Apple watch.

If we subscribe to the logic that Apple dismiss customer insight as unimportant and that the customer does not know what they want, this should be a roaring success. The decision that 'thou shalt have a smart watch' is the absolute epitome of drill based thinking

Apple: Would you like to see an inferior version of what's on the screen of your phone on your watch as well? Oh and bear in mind you'll need to charge your watch every day or it will stop telling the time, requiring you to err..look at the phone in your pocket..

Consumer: No thanks, that sounds stupid!

Apple: If you sat for 2 hours in a focus group, could you eventually be coerced into coming up with some uses for our watch?

Consumer: Well I suppose if you were paying me I could help you justify your watch, but would never actually buy it.

Apple: Great, that is really helpful insight. Lets do it!

Breaking News –Apple Watch was a drill - It's official.

So how have things gone for the Apple Watch since I wrote all this a year ago?

The premium model has been scrapped, the whole positioning has been narrowed from a ubiquitous life changing wearable to a me-too sports watch competing in a mature commoditised market where well established brands compete at a third the price.

Volume for the Apple watch is down 71.6% vs year ago, suggesting that once the fanboys and early adopters ran out, Apple didn't have a story for the mainstream who actually demand some kind of relevance from their products.

And it was all so deeply predictable.

I think there could be a role for smart watches as long as the technology is appropriate, the price is proportionate to the value, the target is focused and the features are relevant. Until then the Apple watch remains the very eitome of a drill looking for a hole.

DRILL BASED

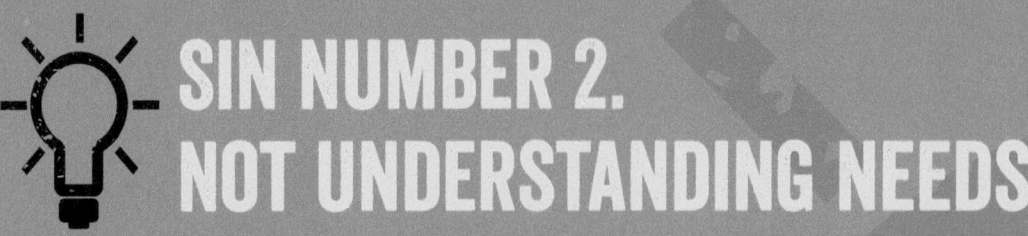

SIN NUMBER 2.
NOT UNDERSTANDING NEEDS

What Archimedes knew about step 21...

We're constantly hearing companies boast that they're 'consumer and insight driven'. In my 10+ years of teaching insight development I've never once visited a company who didn't already think they did it already (usually brilliantly!)

I once visited a famous manufacturer of household goods who showed me a 65 step innovation process (probably developed at enormous cost by McKinsey or such like). It had a process flow that only a NASA PHD could love and at step 21 it mentioned in passing 'Generate Insight'

"Oh" I said, that's the step I'm interested in, what do you actually do at step 21? "Not sure" came the reply.

"Well what did McKinsey tell you to do?" Uncomfortable Silence...

Anyone can create an industrial process for innovation, but step 21 is the killer. Without that little bit of pixie dust, all else is irrelevant.

So how should you generate insights? Well the best place to start is to understand what an insight is in the first place.

The literal definition in the Oxford English dictionary is "The capacity to gain an accurate and deeper understanding of someone or something: An Aha! Or Eureka moment"

Despite this being pretty self-explanatory, most of the time, I'd argue that most companies commit this sin of not understanding needs. Even their insight development experts seem to lack a basic grasp of what they are trying to capture.

Rather than insight we're given observation. For example:

- 'Women take twice as long to call an ambulance after heart attacks"
- 'Obesity is the fastest growing health problem in India'

This use of pithy but ultimately unqualified data points does not even begin to match the dictionary definition of an insight. They show an understanding of what is happening which is often generic and obvious to all competitors, but no deeper understanding of why it is happening.

My understanding of the aforementioned Eureka moment was a reference to when ancient mathematician Archimedes sat in a bath and the water poured over the side.

Now presumably the insight was not the observation that water pours over the side when you sit in the bath. This observation would have been apparent to everyone that had ever sat in a bath surely? That was not new, not a deeper understanding, not an insight...

No, the insight that means we remember Archimedes and his bath millennia later was the first explanation of why it was happening. Namely that the amount of water being displaced was identical to the amount of volume he was taking up.

I've always taught that insights need to contain the 3 W's

What is the customer doing and what is happening (observation)

Why is that happening and what are they trying to achieve (Understanding their behaviour, motivation and needs)

Wow, no competitor has explained that in such depth before

So check the statements that your company or organisation proclaim to be insights. Believe it or not, my research shows that 90% of what companies believe are insights are in fact little more than observations. Don't get caught out at step 21 and help your company create their own Eureka moments.

WHAT, WHY ?

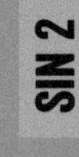

SIN 2 : **NOT UNDERSTANDING NEEDS**
Mistaking observations about what the customer is doing, for insight into why they are doing it.

THE USE OF PITHY BUT ULTIMATELY UNQUALIFIED DATA POINTS DOES NOT EVEN BEGIN TO MATCH THE DICTIONARY DEFINITION OF AN INSIGHT

CASE STUDY SIN #2
 – LUCKY STRIKES CLICK AND ROLL

Not Understanding Needs...

The sin of not understanding real needs is probably the most prevalent indiscretion in the world of innovation.

When thinking of a perfect example, my mind is always drawn to Lucky Strike cigarettes and their recent Click and Roll innovation.

Here's the insight.

You know that moment at the end of a night, when as a non-menthol cigarette smoker, you suddenly feel like becoming a menthol cigarette smoker? No? Of course you do; it happens regularly! So frequently in fact that the proposition of new Lucky Strike 'Click and Roll' is that each of the 20 cigarettes has a menthol capsule built into the filter.

Picture the scene.

At the end of the evening when you want a menthol cigarette instead of your usual smoke, simply squeeze the filter, click the capsule and lo and behold you become a menthol smoker.

What about the 'Roll' you may ask? That's apparently based on the fact that you need to roll the filter between your fingers to activate the flavour (which sounds suspiciously like cover for a design flaw!).

Now apart from the fact that in my experience menthol and non-menthol smokers are two discreet groups who do not abandon their tastes at the end of every evening, there is also the small matter of building a capsule into 20 cigarettes with the clear knowledge that only 1 will ever get used. A slight case of over engineering.

Lets just for a second imagine that there is someone out there that matches the target of a Cinderella style 'midnight menthol convert'

Here's a better proposition.

A single menthol cigarette discreetly built into the base of each pack in case of emergencies. Or even better, a Russian roulette proposition of 1 menthol cigarette randomly disguised in every pack. Now that would add a touch of risk each time you lit up (or perhaps a touch more risk than the core product already delivers!).

This alternative proposition reminds me of a UK chocolate brand called 'Revels' which contains chocolates with mixed centres, (Orange, Toffee, Peanut and Coffee) and it's well known that no-one wants to pick the coffee one.

The manufacturer (Mars) recognises this insight and instead of re-engineering the brand, instead made a unique value proposition which centred around the fun and anticipation of avoiding the coffee ones hidden in the pack.

As the availability and opportunity to use cigarettes is eroded year on year (indeed the EU banned menthol cigarettes in its member states recently), Click & Roll feels like the wrong innovation at the wrong time. Perhaps the owners BAT are too focused on the drill and not the hole, desperate to find ever more obscure ways to push their legacy tobacco technology at unwilling populations.

If they considered new insights and new targets, there could be endless ways to innovate away from cigarettes. The question is whether they really understand how to or truly want to?

PROPOSITION

SIN NUMBER 3.
TRAPPED BY MYTHS AND BELIEFS

Who cares if cats can taste?

When does challenging a preconception or a strongly held customer belief become a Sin? When it prevents us from digging deeper and appreciating what fundamental needs and desires it reveals about the target.

Lets take a simple case in point. Can cats taste?

If you are a cat owner you presumably think so. You'll have experienced that situation where you buy a new brand of cat food only to watch your prized moggy turn up its nose and walk away with a look that says "I'd rather starve than eat that".

However a global pet food manufacturer that I worked with concluded in tests that cats can't discern flavours, only textures. Were they correct? I don't know? Could have been...

Confident in their research, they launched their cat food in three variants 'Kitten, Adult and Senior', but critically not 'Kitten – Beef flavour or Senior – Turkey flavour'.

So how did that work out? Pretty damn badly as it happens.

The product was eventually forced to re-launch with a full complement of the usual cat food flavours in order to survive.

The moral of this story is that the key stakeholder in this particular value chain is the cat owner not the cat. They buy products for their pet based on their own beliefs.

Testimony to this, one of the biggest cat food brands in the UK is named 'Tastes as good as it looks' which comes as a dish of delicious steaklets. Presumably this looks as good as it tastes to a human? If it was the cat, it might look more like a decapitated door mouse. The needs and insight in this market are human driven, hence why in the US, 2.5 million dogs are on prescription anti-depressants, $1 billion was spent last year alone on pet Halloween outfits and consumers admit to spending more on food for their pets than their children.

What lesson can we learn from Sin Number 3? That we don't get to steamroll over customer perceptions or beliefs, just because our solution requires it. We need to empathise with the customer, value their thoughts, reframe them or evolve them, yet we ignore them at our peril.

Dyson are a counterpoint to the cat food manufacturer in question. When faced with the accepted customer belief that 'the more powerful a vacuum cleaner, the more dirt it sucks up.',
they worked with the customers view as a start point.'

Instead of contradicting the customer, they re-phrased the debate to one about the importance of constant suction. "What use is all that power if it stops sucking as the bag fills up?" they said.

The Value Proposition of a cyclonic vacuum cleaner designed not to lose suction, was an elegant solution that disrupted the market.

Far better this approach than that of a client of mine who created the most powerful 2000 watt vacuum cleaner that generated so much suction that it stuck to the carpet and wouldn't move.

In my experience customers hold beliefs for a multitude of legitimate reasons; cultural, historical, experiential. The sophisticated innovator likes their customer. They seeks to understand where their beliefs stem from so they can get closer to revealing the true need. The sinful innovator ignores them and categorises the customer as 'stupid' and 'ill informed' forging ahead with a dissonant solution that will ultimately fail.

EMPATHISE

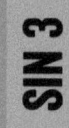

SIN 3
TRAPPED BY MYTHS AND BELIEFS
Ignoring the customers existing habits, rituals and beliefs if they are inconvenient or don't match our solutions.

16

"

WE DON'T GET
TO STEAMROLL
OVER CUSTOMER
PERCEPTIONS OR
BELIEFS JUST BECAUSE
OUR SOLUTION
REQUIRES IT "

CASE STUDY SIN #3 – THE TATA NANO

Trapped by myths and beliefs

In the world of technology innovation, there is one thing guaranteed, that every team has a project entitled 'Value'. Be it a 'Value MR', 'Value TV' or 'Value Robot Spouse', the intention is to create a cheaper, de-featured version of the standard product for developing markets.

There's clearly a few things wrong with that, namely that value is subjective, it doesn't mean the same thing as price, and although their markets are developing, most Indians and Chinese don't see themselves as poor.

Lets take those 3 things one at a time and look at them through the lens of the Tata Nano, a car created by the Indian conglomerate Tata to be the cheapest car in the world.

Clearly value is subjective right? I don't see any reason why someone would pay $6,300 for a pair of Christian Louboutin Multi-Color Crystal-Embellished Pumps for example. Others may wonder why paying $2 million dollars for a supercar that does 0-60 mph in 3 seconds and goes over 200 miles an hour is a wise use of pennies. It takes all sorts.

Clearly value is in the eye of the beholder and mixing the word value with price might lead us to believe that we can define a price that makes anything attractive to everyone.

Finally, as we will come to see clearly in sin number 7 (focusing on function not emotion) , Maslow's hierarchy of needs shows us that it's aspiration and emotional fulfilment that matter most.

Unfortunately it appears that Tata became trapped by their own beliefs about value, and refused to hear any different opinion from their target consumer.

If telling someone that their first car and their single biggest expenditure was going to be universally recognised by everyone they meet as the worlds cheapest, is rather a slap in the face. Implying that this is all they deserve or aspire to because they are poor and undiscerning, is therefore the metaphorical equivalent of a knee in the groin.

Tata also held the view that everyone had to buy a new car, which of course was a failure (or unwillingness) to consider all the alternatives.

For the price of a Nano, someone could easily get a 3 year old "proper Japanese car". Why would the target spend 150,000 INR for a pretend one?

Even functionally the product failed to deliver on its commitments. It couldn't be made for the 100k INR price that Tata originally promised and it famously set on fire, eroding the confidence of the target consumer. The compromises in terms of space and size which were made to create this dirt cheap car meant it was unsuitable for large Indian families.

For some consumers that Tata had in mind for a Nano, a two wheeled alternative such as a scooter or motorcycle actually presented a better proposition of value. For those that were in the market for a car, it failed to take into account their beliefs, their habits or their needs.

Critically in India, not everyone is able to afford a car and it therefore affords the owner an air of exclusivity and becomes a social symbol. That is the value. Any value proposition for a new car needed to appreciate this, unfortunately the Nano did the exact opposite.

ALTERNATIVES

SIN NUMBER 4.
BELIEVING YOU CAN CREATE NEEDS

Why you don't need 6 blades on your razor...

When I began training my insights course, I was led to believe that I needed just one blade on my razor, for that unparalleled close shave. By the time of writing I'm now aware that apparently anything less than 6 is a waste of my time.

My fourth sin of innovation revolves around those who perpetuate false needs in the hope of creating a point of differentiation.

For years, my dishwasher has bleeped at the end of its wash cycle. It's designed to alert me to something, but what?

One premium European dishwasher manufacturer would have us believe we need to open the door when it bleeps. If not the steam remaining in the dishwasher will condense back on to the plates and keep them from drying properly.

Now I'm no engineer, but were this to be remotely true, surely the machine could be fitted with a vent for this purpose. This would prevent the owner being interrupted, or required to hang around in a state of perpetual readiness , to open the door the moment the wash is finished.

However unfettered by this logic, the manufacturer in question has perpetuated that false need by creating an auto-door opening feature across its range. You know, to dry the dishes...

This attempt to create problems that no one knew they had in order to sell something no one needs, surrounds us daily.

In medical systems, nuclear medicine has the slice wars. The more slices a CT makes when imaging the patient the better, first 8 then 16, 32, 64, 128. In only the rarest of cases and procedures is this the critical factor, however it has been so heavily hyped by the industry that it now shrouds all other developments and clinical needs .

In many of these cases, needs are simply created to try and justify useless technologies or to find a point of difference.

Need an egg tray that's internet connected so it can tell you when your eggs are old? Of course you do! Need a bowl that stops your milk splashing out when poured on cornflakes? Think carefully!

"Of course you can create needs", I'm often told when training. "No consumer would ever have asked for the internet!".

This is the ultimate red-herring that is espoused by those who simply don't know or don't care to understand the difference between technologies and benefits.

The consumer would not have asked for the internet, but they would have asked for a dating agency that gave them a greater chance of meeting that certain someone. They would have asked for a way to trade that pinball machine in the garage with someone who valued it, wherever in the world they were.

The internet did not create needs, it facilitated companies and individuals to solve existing needs in a better way. Those needs such as social networking and long distance communication pre-dated the internet. They may have been solved by smoke signals and jungle drums or Marconi and his radio, but the needs were constant.

I believe that good insights endure. They may evolve and become more sophisticated as we do, but we cannot create needs that don't exist and we certainly should not create problems in order to solve them.

FACILITATE

SIN 4
BELIEVING YOU CAN CREATE NEEDS
Deluding yourself that your solution or technology will create new customer needs that don't currently exist.

"WE CANNOT CREATE NEEDS THAT DON'T EXIST AND WE CERTAINLY SHOULD NOT CREATE PROBLEMS IN ORDER TO SOLVE THEM"

CASE STUDY SIN #4 – THE HYUNDAI VELOSTER

Believing you can create needs...

The estimated cost to bring a new car platform to market is half a billion dollars. The average time frame is 5-7 years.

If you were a car manufacturer that was going to spend this much time and money, you'd think that basing the concept on a real unmet consumer need would be essential. You'd also imagine that trying to contrive a problem that doesn't exist, or escalate the significance of a minor one as the cornerstone of your proposition would be ludicrous...

Ladies and gentlemen, I present to you the Hyundai Veloster.

The Tag Line of the Hyundai Veloster commercial is "One Car, Two Sides', the discriminator of the value proposition appears to be that it's the only car in the world stupid enough to have a different number of door on one side compared to the other! But I'm getting a little ahead of myself. Let's step back.

The car in question has a relatively straight forward concept to explain. The designers have removed the rear door behind the driver, but unlike a standard coupe, they have retained the door behind the passenger. Or perhaps they have taken a coupe and added an extra door on the side nearer the kerb. Not sure..

So we know what they've done, but not why they've done it. A value proposition with no insight.

To try and derive an insight that led to this radical and expensive design choice, we need to look at the value proposition they are communicating to potential consumers.

That at least is straightforward. The insight is that car owners fear that passengers in the back will step out onto the road. Therefore the best way to ensure that this does not happen is to entirely remove that door.

But hang on! I've just got a couple of quick questions about that insight.

For who is that the biggest unmet need when choosing a car? Which passengers exactly have this lemming like fixation with moving traffic? What's wrong with child locks? They are present on all cars and can be set independently on each door can't they?

These are big questions and ones that Hyundai seem unable to adequately answer in their value proposition. Is it targeted at taxi drivers? Perhaps at parents of young children? At least that would make sense.

Ah, but that can't be it. You see, Hyundai have styled the car as a boy racer hot hatch back, with high powered turbo charged engines, rear spoilers and a panoplies of blingy alloy wheel choices.

If you're not confused yet, you will be when you see the contradictory communication of the value proposition Hyundai pump out to the market. Sometimes it's the insight about a no compromise coupe aimed at reluctant new fathers 'one side bucket seat, the other baby seat". The next thing you see is terrifying messages about road safety seemingly aimed at Uber drivers who are likely to be dropping off drunk passengers on dark autobahns.

Truth is, Hyundai clearly don't know the insight or the value proposition of the Veloster. They can't define it, can't keep their designers and media agencies aligned to it, can't communicate it.

All we can tell for certain is they've spent a fortune designing a car that's convinced your priority is a non-symmetrical door count? Hope you're clearer now.

AND THE POINT IS?

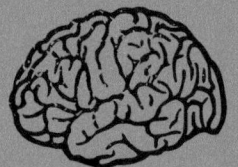

SIN NUMBER 5.
OVERCOMPLICATING STUFF

Why your iron shouldn't call you at work...

Since I started training insight and innovation, my career has been punctuated by run-ins with ludicrously over engineered household appliances.

From vacuum cleaners that you chat with via text, to an oven that bakes your dish as well as your meal. My favourite remains the iron that phones you at work when you leave it on, so you can drive home and switch it off.

I tell that story in all my training sessions, to reinforce why making products purposefully complicated and high tech, can often backfire.

The product team in question had also made an iron which contained an accelerometer, when you didn't pick that one up for more than 3 minutes, it turned itself off. This seemed like an eminently better solution to me, as it was simple, significantly lower effort for the owner and less likely to result in disaster if you changed your phone number without remembering to inform the iron.

However when I asked the developers why they had created this masterstroke of over engineering, they said "because it's the worlds only internet connected iron!" As if that was justification in its own right. "There's probably a good reason for that!" I replied.

I reminded them that the role of innovation is to make the customer look good, not to make the manufacturer look clever!

We need to remind ourselves frequently that the technology in our products is the enabler to the benefit, not the benefit in itself. It doesn't matter how complicated the science is, if the customer doesn't understand it, or worse still if it becomes an obstacle to the customer achieving their desired outcome.

As a counterpoint, I always share with teams the S-Oil campaign from South Korea. The insight was well established that parking spaces are of a premium and that fuel is wasted driving around endlessly looking for one.

Their solution of an arrow shaped balloon in every parking space however was both novel and elegant. When a car enters the space and drives over the string, the attached balloon falls. When the car leaves again the balloon rises, clearly indicating from afar where empty spaces exist within the car park.

Is this solution any less valuable because it doesn't use complicated technology in order to achieve the benefit?

Of course not! Discerning customers evaluate solutions based on how likely they are to be effective and whether the appropriate technology has been applied in a clever way to achieve a meaningful benefit.

I love technology myself, but have learned the discipline of looking at a solution and not focusing on 'How does it do that?', but 'Why does it do that?'

"Ah, but our customer is also a nerd" I often get told by teams trying to defend the indefensible. "They love technology too!", "They are early adopters, who crave gizmos and every possible feature (just in case!)"

The truth is, that one or two customers may fit this profile, but the vast majority do not! If we engineer and specify our solutions to satisfy ourselves and a tiny subset of the target, we endanger disenfranchising and confusing everyone else.

Our mantra should always remain – Benefits first.

WHY DO IT?

SIN 5

OVERCOMPLICATING STUFF
Making something so elaborate and over engineered that it's pointless or impossible to understand and use.

> **THE TECHNOLOGY IN OUR PRODUCTS IS THE ENABLER TO THE BENEFIT, NOT THE BENEFIT IN ITSELF.**

CASE STUDY SIN #5  – THE AIR UMBRELLA

Overcomplicating stuff...

"Any intelligent fool can make things bigger and more complex... It takes a touch of genius - and a lot of courage to move in the opposite direction." The creators of the Air Umbrella would have done well to heed these words!

The Air Umbrella is presented as an 'invisible umbrella' that enables you to pitch wind against water in the quest to stay sheltered from the rain.

In essence, the device consists of a rather clumsy looking stick which contains a lithium battery, which in turn powers a fan. When activated, the 'umbrella' blasts a canopy of air which supposedly deflects rain. A sort of 'force field' to protect you from incoming precipitation attacks too.

Here we have a project that attempts to re-engineer the basic umbrella but does so in such a complicated way that it not only fails to improve on an existing product, but actually adds barriers to the process of sheltering from the rain.

Lets start with its weight. The Air Umbrella weighs around 850 grams, which is almost equivalent to the weight of a large bag of sugar. A little research shows that the average umbrella weighs less than half of that. Perhaps you are thinking that although it's heavier, it must be smaller in dimension than the best alternative? I'm afraid not! The air umbrella is 50cm long, whilst the bestselling folding umbrella on Amazon is only 30cm when you are carrying it around.

So it's both heavier and more bulky than the current alternatives, not something you'd want to carry above your head for long. Maybe this was the reason the creators decided to give his product a relatively short battery life.

Oh yes! Battery life!

Adding insult to injury, the top model only retains enough battery life for 30 minutes of rain dodging, and then you face the hassle of having to re-charge the device. I was under the impression that the whole point of umbrellas (especially the small fold-up ones) was convenience; the ease of being able to quickly grab one from your bag to shelter you from unexpected downpours. What's convenient about a product that constantly needs recharging and where pre-planning is essential?

Interestingly in response to criticism about battery-life , the creator admits the device may be "more suitable for people who have a car". Yes, really!

The Air Umbrella raises a couple of other issues too. Firstly, the device makes use of fan technology to blow the rain away. This will be both noisy and presents the very real risk of blowing rain on to other people. The Umbrella has a splash-zone of 50-70cm away. So anybody in close proximity will get a soaking.

Clearly the well-established alternative design protects the user from the rain in a non anti-social way, allowing the rain to fall safely and inoffensively just to your side.

Refusing to accept they have created complexity out of simplicity, the creators don't seem to think this is a problem; by their logic, if it's raining then other people will have their own umbrellas to protect them from splashback!

Breaking news. The Air Umbrella did overcomplicate stuff: So how have things gone since I wrote this a year ago? Not good I'm afraid. Judging by the tale of woe on Kickstarter. Unhappy investors and an apology by the creators for over engineering their solution means it's all over for the Air Umbrella.

PRACTICAL

SIN NUMBER 6.
BELIEVING YOUR CUSTOMER IS A FOOL

Why Jane Austen didn't have man sized hands...

Carl Jung the famous psychologist once said "If one does not understand a person, one tends to regard him as a fool." This proves to be perhaps more true of those involved in innovation development than anywhere else in life.

A few years ago I was speaking at a conference in Malmo when a member of the audience asked "How do I make my team more insightful?". A co-presenter said the perfect condensed version of everything:- "You can't" he replied "You either recruit curious people or you don't"

So many times over the years I've seen a lack of interest and empathy with the customer manifest itself as a personal attack on them. "Why are they doing that, they must be an idiot?" or "Why are they thinking that, everyone knows that's not true!"

More often than not, the customer is behaving entirely rationally and their behaviour is based on first hand experience. It's our frustration that we don't understand them or why they don't want our pointless innovations that's actually so galling.

A perfect example I encountered recently was a project involving a voice controlled device. "Just speak to it and tell it what to do" I was told by the development team.

Based on my extensive experience of failing to get voice commands to work in my car, on my phone and with my telephone bank I tried it apprehensively. Low and behold it didn't work at all. Quel surprise!

"You are not speaking clearly enough", "Try talking in a place with less background noise" , "You're not pronouncing the words with the correct sibilance!" – Sibilance?

When I pointed out that in the real world they would not be able to dictate the precise sibilance of the users voice, they were not having it. Instead they insisted that their product was perfect and it was the user that must be at fault and would need to change.

The other way in which this lack of respect for the customer manifests itself is through the repeated use of patronising stereotypes.

Can't be bothered to find real insight into how women's attitudes and needs differ from men? No worries just patronise them with the exact same product coloured pink!

Disinterested in how men's roles are evolving in parenting and housework? Don't stress! Continue to develop male products that assume low interest and low effort are the order of the day.

I never cease to be amazed by how lack of insight into the customer turns rapidly into lack of respect. I once saw a Russian Sat Nav designed for women, that alongside being the obligatory pink, also had tailored voice prompts. These included "Slow down, you don't want to ruin that hair" and "Are you sure you want to go there? Such a lot of traffic!"

One brand manager once told me "I don't own a TV" she said, "I think it's for the plebs".

"Those plebs" I replied "are your customers". "I think that liking your customer should be a basic job requirement".

I've come to learn that a non insightful manager keeps busy in the office all day looking busy. An insightful manager gets out of the office and immerses themselves in the lives and jobs of their customers. As managers we need to reinforce the behaviours of those curious ones, the ones that judge less and care more.

INSIGHTFUL

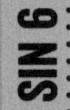

SIN 6
BELIEVING YOUR CUSTOMER IS A FOOL
Labelling your customer as stupid or irrational if they ask for something that conflicts with what you are selling.

> **"I NEVER CEASE TO BE AMAZED BY HOW LACK OF INSIGHT INTO THE CUSTOMER TURNS RAPIDLY INTO LACK OF RESPECT "**

CASE STUDY SIN #6 – RYAN AIR AND BIC CRYSTAL FOR HER

Believing your customer is a fool…

It's easy to assume your customer is a fool. Take Ryan Air the low cost European airline for example.

Their controversial boss Michael O'Leary made a career of sneering at and belittling his own customers. His belief was that his airlines product was so brilliant that no amount of bad experience would put passengers off. Rude staff, yes, rugby scrum for your seat, yes, separated from your kids all the way to an airstrip a coach ride from your real destination, tick again. So what was this brilliant value proposition? It seems Mr O'Leary just like Tata with its Nano, mistook the term value for price. He too believed that his customers would accept a poor, demeaning product as long as it was cheap.

When it came to the sin of taking their customer for a fool, Ryan Air excelled. They submitted applications for pay toilets on their planes and new 'seats' that required the passengers to stand up for the entirety of the flight. Mr O'Leary clearly despised his customers with a passion rarely seen before or since.

But my sins of innovation are immutable, just like the laws of physics. Very soon, Ryan Air's market share and passenger numbers were nose-diving.

Cue a road to Damascus moment at the O'Leary household. Last year Mr O'Leary apologised to shareholders and admitted that the airline should 'try to eliminate things that unnecessarily piss people off'.

What, no! trying to actively respect your customers and not purposefully put your own interests before theirs? Surely not. This reminds me of another spectacular misjudged innovation from Bic Biro's. How could you get pen innovation wrong you may think? Well they managed it, and with style too!

The first mistake Bic Made was to create a pen for women, without gaining any true insight into the fore-mentioned gender. As women make up half the world, you don't have to go very far before bumping into one. Although I have to say that understanding women takes life long dedication and focus!

Bic's value proposition for the 'Bic Crystal for Her' seems to be predicated on the 'insight' that women have small hands. Oh yes!

This is followed up by the fact that Bic Crystal pens also allow women to write 2 times more words than normal 'man pens' would allow. What are you implying Bic?

Amazon who are selling the pens have received a tide of critical and sarcastic reviews including the following gems:

"As the father of three daughters and husband of one wife, for many years I have been irritated at how often I have had to field complaints about how my pens were not suited for the other members of my household. Now, at last, Bic has supplied the solution. I am SO grateful. And the pink colour is PERFECT! EVERYONE knows how much ALL women just LOVE pink. Well done, Bic, I am about to order a lifetime supply and stop all the whining in my house for good."

"At last, a pen for me to hold without fear of collapse and injury. No more accusatory looks from hospital staff when I explain that my sprained wrist occurred while writing a shopping list with my man pen."

And my favourite…. "How on earth did J K Rowling and Agatha Cristie and Jane Austen manage without!? They must have had awfully big mans hands. Can't wait for the hubby to come home and show me how to work it." It beggars belief how manufacturers can be so superficial and so insulting to their customers all at the same time.

EMPATHISE

SIN NUMBER 7.
FOCUSING ON FUNCTION NOT EMOTION

Why you shouldn't mention whale vomit on valentines...

In Scandinavia people walk up and down the beaches searching for rocks called ambergris. If they find some, a guy flies in from Paris in a helicopter and buys it from them, there and then, for hundreds of thousands of dollars.

Ambergris is a gall stone vomited out by a whale which then washes up on a surrounding beach. More intriguingly, it's the core component of many fine fragrances (hence the eager Frenchman with the cheque book!) Despite the industries best efforts, you can't synthesise the unique smell of ambergris in a lab! Oh no! You need real whale vomit!

Am I making you feel more inclined to buy expensive perfume, now I'm explaining how it's made? Does its value escalate because I've revealed how it works and what's in it?

Of course not. As Maslow said so succinctly 80 years ago we value emotion far higher than function. You don't want me telling you the value proposition of fine fragrance by describing how it works, but instead how it will make you feel!

Don't tell me about whale vomit, show me Nicole Kidman swooping up the steps of the Moulin Rouge!

Don't be deceived, this principle is just as true for technology and B2B components as it is a for fashion brands and consumer products. If it weren't we all would be buying Samsung tablets, not iPads. Spec for spec they are functionally very similar (indeed Samsung probably makes many key components in the iPad).

Instead we are drawn to the brands and value propositions that can explain how we are going to feel. We want to hear how cool we will look or how much more expertly we will do our jobs.

It's no accident that the tag line for BMW remains 'The ultimate driving machine' rather than the 'ultimate machine'. BMW have understood for years that the driving experience is the hero of their value proposition. It's the 'Joy' of driving that's at the forefront, not the anti lock breaks, limited slip differential and adaptive suspension.

Whenever I'm training insights and value propositions, I teach the use of the 'so what test'. It's a simple device that ensures the product team ask themselves why something exists, rather than simply telling us that it does.

'It's a laptop charging cable that's magnetic', -'So what? 'Well it doesn't use a pin plug like all other competitors',- So what? 'Well if you trip over the cable it safely disconnects' – So what? 'You can always be confident your treasured laptop won't fall and smash' – Ah now that's a benefit!

But aren't there some customers who are only interested in how a product works? No! It's critical that we don't characterise our customer as uniquely dispassionate and devoid of emotion. I regularly hear people tell me that the radiologist or anaesthetist they develop for is a soulless function freak. This is nonsense.

Someone once told me that there is no environment more than a hospital where someone is likely to ask 'How do you feel?'

Naturally if we interact with our customers in a purely functional way, they will respond accordingly. However they are human beings, that use their emotions to make decisions both inside and outside of work. Spend just five minutes with an oncologist talking about what satisfaction looks like in their job, rather than trying to push technology on them and my point will become instantly obvious.

CONFIDENT

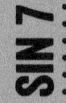

SIN 7 : **FOCUSING ON FUNCTION NOT EMOTION**
Thinking that the technology & how your solution works is the value your customer receives rather than what it enables them to do.

"OUR CUSTOMERS USE THEIR EMOTIONS TO MAKE DECISIONS BOTH INSIDE AND OUTSIDE OF WORK "

CASE STUDY SIN #7 – LG HOMECHAT

Focusing on function not emotion...

With the arrival of the 'Internet of Things', we now seem to be living in a truly 'smart' environment, with developers fighting tooth and nail to contribute to the 'nu-generation' of connected products.

And while this presents us with some exciting ideas, it undoubtedly opens up the floodgates for a barrage of pointless innovations that serve no real function and are so devoid of emotional benefit Maslow would spin in his grave.

The Egg Minder internet connected egg tray is a perfect example of this. It is aimed at the consumer market, for the purpose of monitoring a) how many eggs are left in the fridge and b) whether these eggs are still fit to be eaten. And what's more, it'll text you or email you to tell you its findings.

The Egg Minder features a built-in Wi-Fi chip that enables the device to sync with a user's phone / tablet, via the Wink app. Once eggs are placed in the LED lights will indicate the age of each egg (based only on when they were placed into the tray, -not how long ago they were laid), while push notifications will provide a running commentary when eggs are 'on the turn' or stocks are running low.

Are you following this?

Pointless internet connected propositions are rife but LG has bettered them all. They have created a complete ecosystem called Homechat that allows consumers to interact with and hold conversations with their household appliances via the web.

So what kind of things could you do if you owned an LG Homechat Appliance?

Well according to LG, you could send your robotic vaccuum cleaner a text message to inform it that you will be 30 minutes late home from work. It will then delay the cleaning of your floors for that additional half an hour, to ensure that it completes its duties and parks itself away only at the moment you come through the door.

And the emotional benefit of all that function? Well, that's clear right? Who would feel reassured or relaxed thinking of that additional 30 minutes of dust accumulating while you commute home late? It's bad enough the stress of working late, who needs the crippling worry of that extra dust?

How about telling your washing machine to finish it's wash cycle at that moment too? What better way to relax when getting in late than the knowledge you have to immediately hang out your washing that just couldn't wait?

The world is full of value propositions built on useless function. Want to take photographs with the phone in your pocket and upload them to the cloud? Do you want the resolution to be high enough your picture could decorate the external façade of a department store? You do? Good, then you need the 41 megapixel Lumia smartphone with its 7500x 5500 pixel pictures.

Need to know exactly what time and pressure you applied to each individual tooth when you last cleaned your teeth? You do? Then you need the bluetooth 4.0 connected Oral B Smart Series electric toothbrush.

There's a simple rule, that applies to all my case studies in this book. People buy benefits, not technology. Perhaps I should make an app to send push notifications to product teams each time they forget. Now that is a great value proposition!

EMOTIONAL BENEFIT

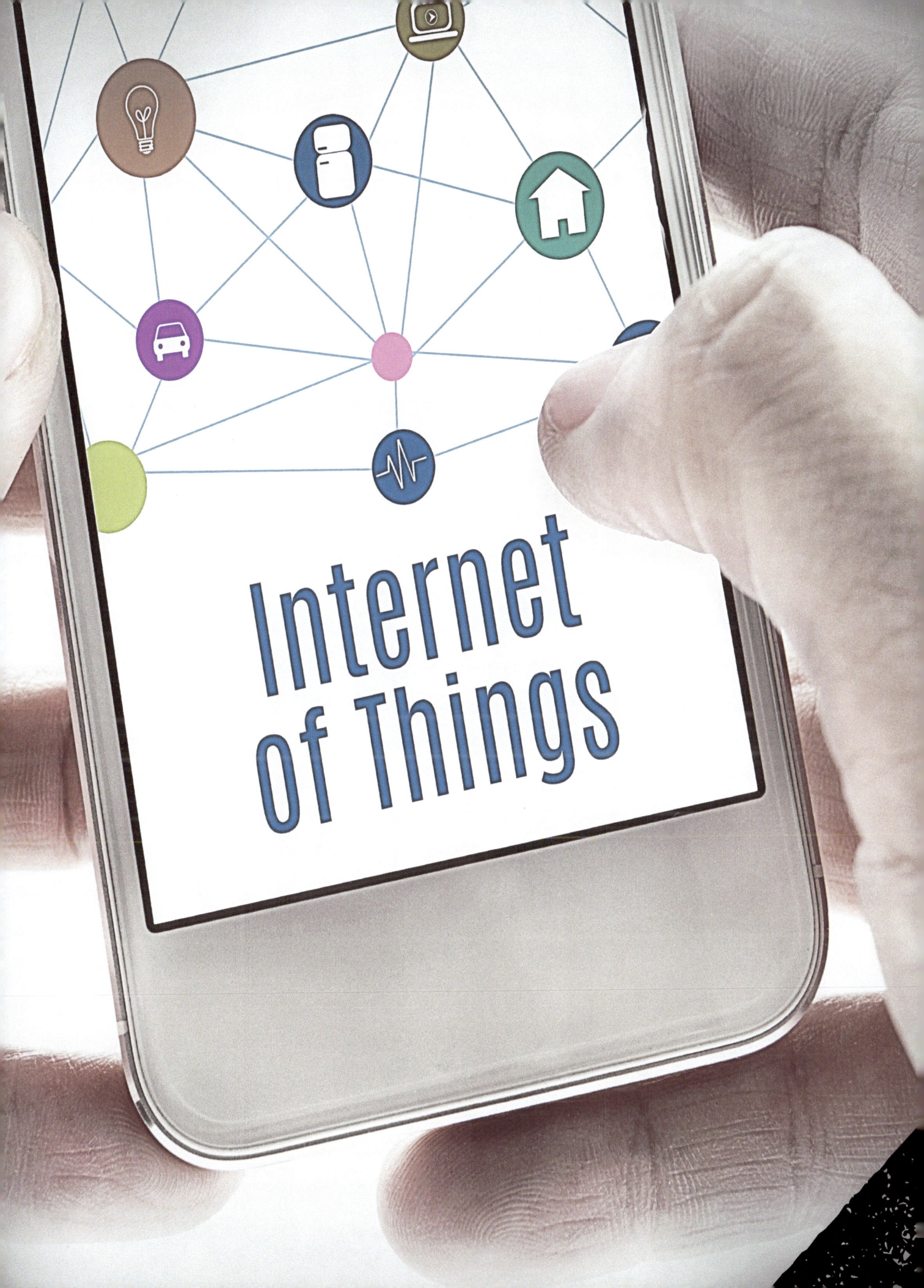

INNOVATION SAINT – THE AUTO DISABLE LIFE SAVER SYRINGE

Simple solutions to real problems...

With all this talk of innovation sinners, it's really quite nice to end this book by looking at what happens when someone considers customer insights. There are a multitude of innovation saints out there, both in B2C and B2B businesses.

My favourite story is a remarkably simple piece of technology which avoids sin number 5 (overcomplicating things) beautifully. Although developed as a concept over 30 years ago, it has garnered significant press attention recently due to support by the World Health Organisation.

The innovation is the LifeSaver Syringe (also known as the K1 Auto-Disable Syringe) –a self-destructing needle & syringe combo that has the potential to halt the spread of blood-borne infections, particularly within developing countries:

British charity worker Marc Koska first came up with the idea for a 'smart syringe' in the mid-1980s. After reading a newspaper article about the predicted spread of HIV and AIDS as a direct result of syringe re-use during routine procedures (often by medical practitioners), Marc set to work creating a solution to this very real global problem. He started from a real problem thus avoiding both sin number 1 (pushing not pulling) and sin number 5 (creating needs)

As Marc knew what doctors were doing, but not why they were doing it he set about talking to medical practitioners in developing countries, avoiding sin 2 (not understanding their needs). In doing this Marc found that lack of funds led people to reuse needles, not a cavalier attitude to the health of patients.

His empathy for why they acted as they did prevented him from labelling them as foolish and simply relying on the existing solution and yet another education campaign (sin number 6).

He needed to acknowledge their existing behaviour and motivations and evolve how they worked by providing a better solution, therefore not being trapped by existing myths and beliefs (sin number 3.)

His motivation and communication of the story was simple: stop re-use, stop infection and save lives (emotion not function)

His value proposition was even simpler: How can you ensure a syringe won't be used again? Reason to Believe - a syringe that can't be re-used.

Marc designed the K1 Auto-Disable Syringe so that, following single usage, the plunger cannot be pulled back. If the user attempts to re-load, the syringe will break.

It was important that the product and material be engineered to keep the price low, so that single use syringes would not be rejected on their economics.

So, what makes the K1 such a good innovation? It took real observations and turned them into insight, then a really simple and compelling value proposition

STATISTIC: "Every year, 20 million HIV positive syringes are re-used in Africa"

STATISTIC: "17 billion injections are given each year. 7 billion are unsafe"

STATISTIC: "1.3 million people a year are killed by syringe re-use"

The K1 Auto-Disable Syringe ticks all of these boxes; a simple solution, firmly driven by insight and one now endorsed by the World Health Organisation as the future of all syringes by 2020.

MOTIVATION

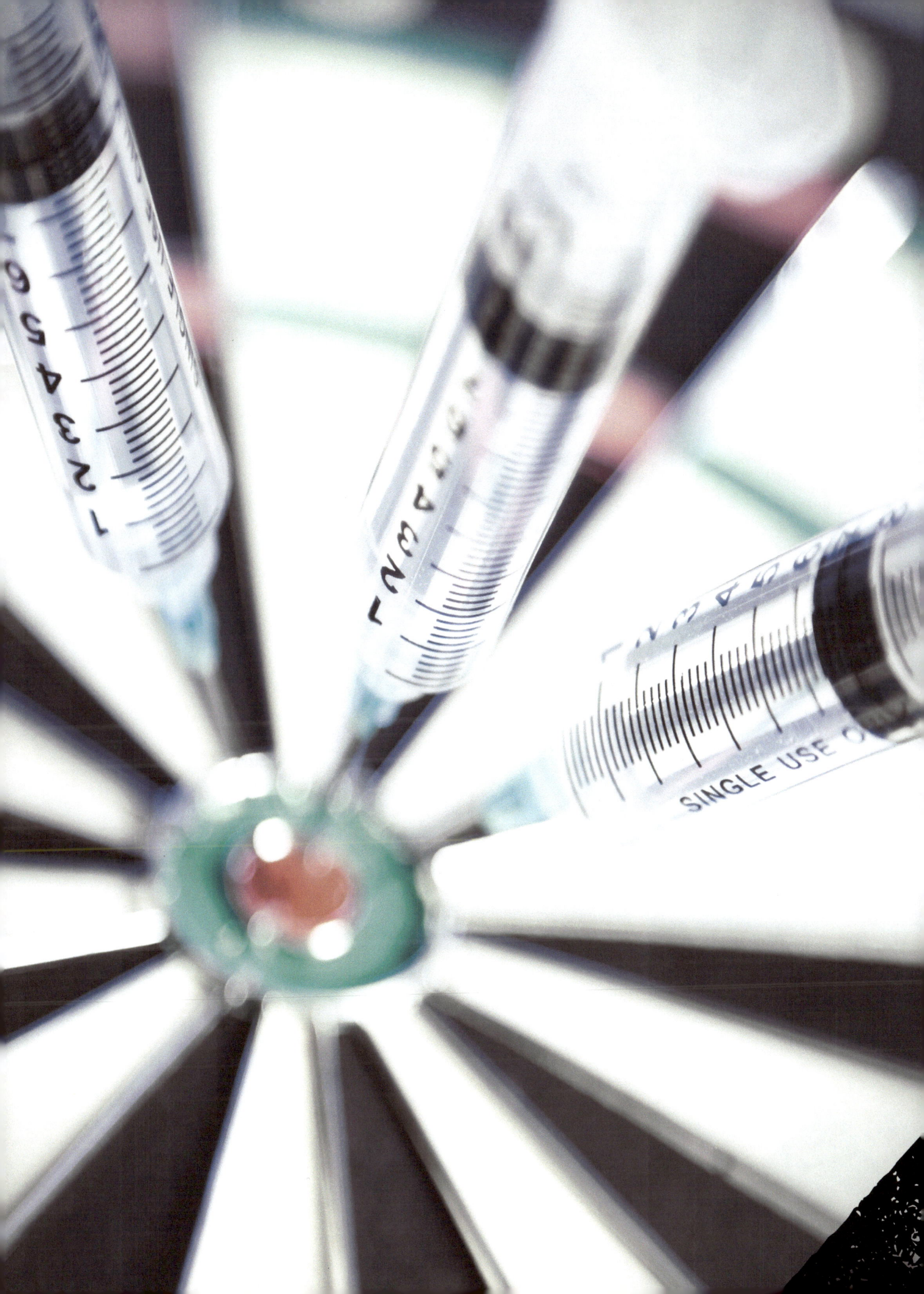

THE HEAVENLY 6 BLOCKER

Building for future success...

Since I started Outside In™ back in 2003, I've been teaching people all over the world how to create and develop better insights and value propositions.

In that time I've refined and perfected a simple 6 Block Grid which forms a thinking framework to help write brilliant value propositions. This isn't something I invented, it's based on best practice used throughout the industry.

Perhaps it's because I've kept it simple, perhaps it's because it really works or perhaps its because we solve a real insight, but the 6 Block approach goes from strength to strength each year.

I'm proud to say that as I write this, nearly 250,000 employees in some of the worlds biggest companies use my method and tools as part of their daily job.

Our philosophy at Outside In™ is 'Seeing and Doing is Believing'.

We know that insight driven innovation and value proposition creation may not have been the historical culture of our clients. We regularly meet and consult with highly intelligent people who need persuading that such a shift is appropriate for them.

As a result we build all our methods on a series of case studies close to the day to day situation of our clients. We prove through showing example after example that the move to insight driven innovation is not only achievable but highly desirable for those we train

This constantly evolving use of up to date products and examples to illustrate our learning objectives prevents the Outside in (TM) workshops becoming reliant on dry theory and keeps them interactive and engaging.

That's why our workshops have such unprecedented word of mouth recommendation and has been proven to change the culture of huge established companies where others had failed.

Unlike other large consulting agencies, we do not develop anything other than insight and value propositions for our clients. No PowerPoint for beginners or Finance for non financial managers here.

This complete specialism on one area means we are experts in this field and repeatedly exposed to new examples and ideas every day.

We believe that training and consulting go hand in hand, so our consultants are able to train business groups and project teams 'on the go' as they develop live projects.

The ability to create live action workshops as part of innovation development is a unique benefit of Outside In™ and means that teams get to apply their learning immediately but also develop the skills to replicate this all again in the future. Unlike other consultancies, we want your team to learn to do this for themselves when we've left!

If teams come away from workshops and meetings not only armed with the competency to create better insights and value propositions in the future, but also the groundwork of a real project then we believe that is highly desirable.

As we focus on technology and B2B companies, you'll find as many engineers, designers, programmers and scientists in our sessions as marketers. Our greatest advocates are often the very technical people that used to think marketing people were flighty guys in suits who lacked discipline or focus.

We can teach your multifunctional team of up to 20 in a couple of days how to generate insights and create value propositions. The cost is probably lower than you think and the return can be unlimited. Why not get in touch and talk to us about training your team?

We can be contacted on +44 7961 96 9997 or at info@outsideincompany.com. Give us a call to discuss your needs.

INNOVATION

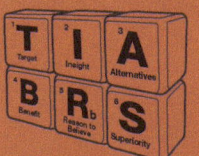

6 BLOCK – VALUE PROPOSITION

1 T Target

Who are we innovating for?

Which segment of the population are you targeting? Think about attitudes as well as demographics.

2 I Insight

What unmet need or dilemma are we addressing?

This should be written in 3 sections:

1. Situation - who am I? What is my context?
   What is going on around me?
2. Dilemma - How does the above situation cause a problem for me? What is the unmet need or trade-off?
3. Perfection - how would you like the world to look?

3 A Alternatives

Who else attempts to address this unmet need or dilemma? Why do they fail?

This box should outline the key direct competitors and indirect competitors their claims and how they currently fail to address the insight.

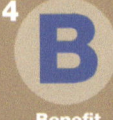

4 B Benefit

The information in this box describes the advantage of this proposition.

The benefit should be a promise to solve the insight. As a result there should only be one single minded rational benefit linked to the emotional reward the target will receive as a result.

5 Rb Reason to Believe

The information in this box describes how you intend to prove the proposition will deliver the benefit.

This can be a combination of technical data, endorsements, testimonials, statistics , and an explanation of how the technology works.

6 S Superiority

The information in this box describes how your proposition is better at solving the insight than competitors.

This should be a single sentence that sums up the superior value of this proposition.

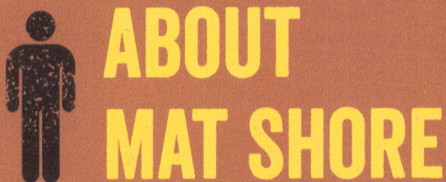

ABOUT
MAT SHORE

The man...

Mat has an infectious passion for innovation. His ability to explain and encourage new thinking in innovation has led to him being invited to train thousands of people in North America, Latin America, Africa, Asia and Europe over the last 11 years.

His material on innovation has been delivered to over 35,000 people worldwide. He has refined and championed a 6 Block Value Proposition approach that is so simple and intuitive to use that it's now best practice in companies with a combined turnover of $150 billion worldwide.

This focus on making value proposition and insight writing accessible has led to Mat developing technology of his own. His Proposition Engine software actually helps teams master the skill of writing and capturing great insights and product concepts.

In 2013 Mat was asked to be the key note speaker at the PMA conference in New Orleans, one of the worlds largest conferences with 20,000 attendees, In this speech he delivered his 7 Deadly Sins speech to great acclaim. You can see a clip from his key note on his website matshore.com.

Mat's unique humour and irreverence means his weekly blog on topical innovation success and failure is viewed by thousands. His opinion is also regularly sought by business publications and newspapers. In 2015 Mat was interviewed by the Times on his thoughts about bad innovation and how he would improve the quality.

In 2003 Mat founded Outside In™, a successful Innovation and Training company which helps clients worldwide challenge their preconceived ideas on insights, propositions and innovation. In the last 11 years, Outside in have consulted on B2B and B2C innovations in 27 countries. As a result Mat has one or two frequent flyer miles.

Mat has worked on countless innovation projects with market leaders such as GE, Philips, Citrix, Electrolux, Samsung, Lafarge, Carestream, AON, Belkin, Gemalto and Analogic .He has also worked with service providers, agencies, universities and start ups. Mat's extensive expertise in this area led to him being asked to train the MBA faculty at Washington University in Insight and proposition development.

Apart from his training and public speaking talents, Mat has many years experience actually running live innovation projects.

In his career Mat has worked across diverse markets, from launching new coffee machines to neo natal MRI scanners. He is a world leading expert in synthesising insights, generating propositions and moderating customer and consumer work.

However it is Mat's humour and ability to transfer knowledge to marketers and engineers alike that makes him so successful. As a leading authority in coaching and developing innovation he'll always find a relevant and motivating example to inspire your team to new breakthrough thinking.

Subscribe to Mats' YouTube channel –MatShoreInnovation or follow him on Linked In for up to date case studies.

Mat Shore
Mat Shore
Marketing Consultant

EXPERIENCE
KNOWLEDGE
INSPIRING

Notes...